Social Media: Unleash the Power of Digital Marketing

Isaac Medina

Published by KNI Publishing Inc, 2024.

While every precaution has been taken in the preparation of this book, the publisher assumes no responsibility for errors or omissions, or for damages resulting from the use of the information contained herein.

SOCIAL MEDIA: UNLEASH THE POWER OF DIGITAL MARKETING

First edition. March 5, 2024.

ISBN: 979-8224865802

Written by Isaac Medina.

Table of Contents

Introduction:

Welcome to the digital revolution! In today's fast-paced world, the landscape of marketing is constantly evolving, and there's no denying the power of social media. From connecting with friends and family to discovering new products and services, social media has become an integral part of our daily lives, shaping the way we communicate, consume content, and make purchasing decisions.

But here's the thing – social media isn't just for scrolling through cat videos or sharing memes anymore. It's a dynamic and ever-expanding platform that presents endless opportunities for businesses to reach and engage with their target audience in ways never before possible. Whether you're a small startup or a global corporation, harnessing the power of social media can catapult your brand to new heights and drive unprecedented growth and success.

That's where this ebook comes in. Titled "Social Media: Unleash the Power of Digital Marketing," this concise, straight to the point, no-nonsense guide is your ticket to unlocking the full potential of social media as a powerful marketing tool. Packed with actionable strategies, expert insights, and real-world examples, this ebook will equip you with the knowledge and skills you need to navigate the complex world of social media marketing with confidence and finesse.

But why should you care about social media marketing, you ask? Well, let me paint you a picture.

Imagine having the ability to reach millions of potential customers with just the click of a button. Imagine being able to target your advertising efforts with laser-like precision, ensuring that your message reaches the right people at the right time. Imagine building a loyal community of brand advocates who sing your praises to anyone who will listen. And imagine seeing tangible results – increased brand awareness, higher website traffic, and a boost in sales and revenue – all thanks to your strategic use of social media.

Sound too good to be true? It's not. With the right knowledge and approach, you can harness the immense power of social media to achieve your business goals and take your brand to the next level.

In this ebook, we'll cover everything you need to know to become a social media marketing maven. We'll start by laying the groundwork with an overview of the current social media landscape, including popular platforms and emerging trends. From there, we'll dive deep into the nitty-gritty details, exploring topics like understanding your target audience, creating compelling content, leveraging influencers, and measuring success.

But this ebook isn't just about theory – it's about action. Each chapter is jam-packed with practical tips, step-by-step guides, and real-world examples that you can apply to your own social media marketing efforts right away. Whether you're a seasoned marketer looking to up your game or a total newbie just dipping your toes into the waters of social media, there's something here for everyone.

So, are you ready to unleash the power of digital marketing and take your brand to new heights? If so, grab a cup of coffee, cozy up in your favorite spot, and let's dive into the exciting world of social media marketing together. The journey starts now – and the possibilities are endless. Let's make magic happen!

Chapter 1:
Understanding the
Social Media
Landscape

A Peek into the Ever-Evolving Landscape

Hey there! Welcome to the wild world of social media. Whether you're a seasoned pro or just dipping your toes in, it's essential to stay up-to-date with the latest trends and platforms. So, let's take a stroll through the current social media landscape and see what's shaking things up.

Meet the Giants:

First up, we've got the heavyweights of social media – Facebook, Instagram, Twitter, LinkedIn, and YouTube. Facebook remains the kingpin, with billions of active users sharing everything from family photos to viral memes. Instagram, with its visually stunning feed and Stories, has become a playground for creatives and influencers alike. Twitter continues to reign supreme in the world of real-time updates and trending conversations, while LinkedIn remains the go-to platform for professionals looking to network and advance their careers. And let's not forget about YouTube, the ultimate destination for video content of all kinds, from tutorials to vlogs to music videos.

The Rising Stars:

But the social media landscape isn't just about the tried-and-true platforms. We've also got some rising stars making waves. TikTok burst onto the scene a few years back and quickly became a global sensation, captivating users with its short-form videos and endless scroll of entertainment. Snapchat, with its disappearing messages and AR filters, continues to appeal to younger audiences seeking a more private and playful social experience. And then there's Pinterest, the virtual pinboard for all things inspiration, from home decor to fashion to recipes.

Emerging Trends:

Now, let's talk about the exciting stuff – emerging trends that are shaping the future of social media. One trend that's been gaining traction is the rise of ephemeral content. Platforms like Instagram Stories, Snapchat, and even Twitter Fleets are capitalizing on the fleeting nature of content, encouraging users to share in-the-moment updates and behind-the-scenes glimpses of their lives. Then there's the growing importance of social commerce, with platforms like Instagram and Facebook rolling out shopping features that allow users to buy products without ever leaving the app. And let's not forget about the rise of video content, with short-form videos dominating feeds and livestreaming becoming more popular than ever.

The Bottom Line:

So, what's the takeaway from all this? The social media landscape is vast, diverse, and constantly evolving. Whether you're a brand looking to connect with your audience, an influencer building your personal brand, or just an everyday user looking to stay connected with friends and family, there's something for everyone in the world of social media. So, strap in, stay curious, and get ready to explore all that this ever-changing landscape has to offer.

Knowing Your Fans: Understanding Your Audience Matters

So, you've got a killer product or service, and you're ready to conquer the social media world. But before you dive headfirst into the deep end, there's one crucial step you can't afford to skip: understanding your audience.

Why Understanding Your Audience Matters:

Think of your audience as the North Star guiding your social media journey. Understanding who they are, what they like, and how they behave is essential for creating content that resonates and drives engagement. After all, you wouldn't try to sell snow to Eskimos, right?

Getting Inside Their Heads:

So, how do you go about understanding your audience? It all starts with research, my friend. Dive deep into demographics like age, gender, location, and income to get a clear picture of who your audience is. But don't stop there – dig into psychographics, too. What are their interests, hobbies, values, and pain points? The more you know, the better you can tailor your messaging and content to speak directly to their hearts (and wallets).

Finding Your Tribe:

Now that you've got a solid grasp on who your audience is, it's time to figure out where they hang out online. Different platforms attract different demographics and serve different purposes, so it's crucial to select the ones that align best with your audience and business goals.

Choosing the Right Platforms:

Let's break it down, shall we? If your audience skews younger and more visually oriented, platforms like Instagram and TikTok might be your best bet. They're all about eye-catching visuals and bite-sized content that's perfect for capturing attention in a scroll-happy world. On the other hand, if you're targeting professionals or B2B clients, platforms like LinkedIn might be more up your alley. It's the go-to spot for networking, thought leadership, and sharing industry insights.

Testing the Waters:

Of course, selecting the right platforms is as much an art as it is a science. It might take some trial and error to figure out which ones resonate most with your audience and drive the best results for your business. Don't be afraid to experiment, track your performance metrics, and adjust your strategy as needed. Remember, Rome wasn't built in a day – and neither is a successful social media presence.

The Bottom Line:

Understanding your audience and selecting the right platforms for your business are like the peanut butter and jelly of social media marketing – they just belong together. By taking the time to get to know your audience and choosing the platforms that best align with their preferences and behaviors, you'll set yourself up for success and pave the way for meaningful connections and engagement. So, roll up your sleeves, grab your magnifying glass, and get ready to dive deep into the world of your audience's wants and needs. It's time to make some magic happen!

Secrets Tips for Market Research and Competitor Analysis

Ready to take your game to the next level? Well, you're in luck because we're diving into the world of market research and competitor analysis – the secret sauce behind any successful social media strategy.

Why Market Research Matters:

Before you can craft a killer social media strategy, you need to understand the lay of the land. Market research is like your trusty map, guiding you through the twists and turns of the digital landscape and helping you uncover hidden gems that'll set you apart from the competition.

Getting Started:

So, where do you begin? Start by defining your goals. What are you hoping to achieve with your social media strategy? Increased brand awareness? More leads? Higher sales? Once you've got your goals in place, it's time to roll up your sleeves and get down to business.

Know Your Audience Inside and Out:

First things first, you need to get to know your audience better than you know the lyrics to your favorite song. Dive deep into demographics like age, gender, location, and income, but don't stop there. Explore psychographics, too – what are their interests, hobbies, values, and pain points? The more you know, the better you can tailor your messaging and content to resonate with them on a deeper level.

Spying on the Competition:

Next up, it's time to play detective and scope out the competition. Take a peek at what your competitors are up to on social media. What platforms are they using? What types of content are they sharing? How often are they posting? But don't just stop at the surface – dig deeper to uncover what's working for them and what's not. What are their strengths and weaknesses? What gaps can you fill in the market?

Tools of the Trade:

Luckily, you don't have to go full-on Sherlock Holmes to gather all this intel. There are plenty of tools out there to help you conduct market research and competitor analysis more efficiently. From social media analytics platforms like Sprout Social and Hootsuite to SEO tools like SEMrush and Ahrefs, there's no shortage of resources at your disposal.

Stay Flexible and Keep Learning:

Remember, market research and competitor analysis aren't one-and-done tasks. The digital landscape is constantly evolving, and what works today might not work tomorrow. Stay flexible, keep an eye on emerging trends, and be willing to pivot your strategy as needed. And don't forget to keep learning and experimenting – the best social media strategies are always evolving.

The Bottom Line:

Market research and competitor analysis are the foundation of any successful social media strategy. By taking the time to understand your audience and scope out the competition, you'll gain invaluable insights that'll inform every aspect of your strategy, from content creation to platform selection to campaign optimization. So, grab your magnifying glass and get ready to uncover the secrets that'll set your social media strategy apart from the rest. It's time to make some magic happen!

A Guide to Clear and Achievable Social

Media Goals

Want to chart a course for success? Well, you've come to the right place because we're about to embark on a journey to setting clear and achievable goals for your social media marketing efforts.

Why Goals Matter:

Setting goals is like plotting a course on your treasure map – it gives you direction and purpose. Without clear goals, you'll be adrift in a sea of content without a compass to guide you. So, let's hoist the sails and get started!

Start with the Basics:

First things first, you need to define what success looks like for your social media strategy. What are you hoping to achieve? Increased brand awareness? More website traffic? Higher engagement? Take some time to brainstorm and jot down your goals – no idea is too big or too small at this stage.

Make Them SMART:

Now that you've got your goals laid out, it's time to make them SMART – Specific, Measurable, Achievable, Relevant, and Time-bound. Instead of saying you want to "increase engagement," get specific – how much engagement are you aiming for? By when? And how will you measure it? Making your goals SMART gives them teeth and makes them easier to track and achieve.

Break It Down:

Once you've got your SMART goals in place, it's time to break them down into smaller, bite-sized chunks. Think of these as your mini-milestones along the way to achieving your bigger goals. Breaking your goals down into smaller tasks makes them feel more manageable and less daunting.

Track Your Progress:

Now that you've got your goals set, it's important to track your progress along the way. Keep a close eye on key performance indicators (KPIs) like engagement rates, follower growth, website traffic, and conversion rates. Use social media analytics tools to monitor your performance and make adjustments to your strategy as needed.

Stay Flexible and Adapt:

Remember, the social media landscape is constantly changing, and what works today might not work tomorrow. Stay flexible and be willing to adapt your goals and strategy as needed. If you're not seeing the results you hoped for, don't be afraid to pivot and try something new. The key is to keep experimenting, learning, and evolving.

Celebrate Your Victories:

Finally, don't forget to celebrate your victories along the way! Whether it's hitting a milestone number of followers, achieving a record-breaking engagement rate, or reaching a new sales goal, take the time to pat yourself on the back and acknowledge your hard work. After all, every step forward is a step closer to reaching your ultimate destination.

The Bottom Line:

Setting clear and achievable goals is the compass that will guide your social media journey and help you navigate the choppy waters of the digital landscape. By making your goals SMART, breaking them down into smaller tasks, tracking your progress, staying flexible, and celebrating your victories along the way, you'll set yourself up for success and chart a course to social media greatness. So, hoist the anchor, set sail, and let's make some waves together!

Chapter 2: Crafting Compelling Content for Social Media

The Heart of Social Media Success

Content creator extraordinaire! Ready to unlock the secrets to capturing your audience's attention and keeping them coming back for more? Well, you're in luck because we're diving deep into the importance of creating engaging and share-worthy content that'll make your audience stop scrolling and start engaging.

Why Engaging Content Matters:

Picture this: you're scrolling through your social media feed, and suddenly, something catches your eye. It's a funny meme, an inspiring quote, or a stunning photo that stops you in your tracks. That, my friend, is the power of engaging content. It's the secret sauce that turns passive scrollers into active participants and transforms casual followers into loyal fans.

Standing Out in a Sea of Noise:

Let's face it – the internet is a noisy place. With millions of pieces of content vying for attention every second, standing out can feel like an uphill battle. But fear not! Engaging content is your secret weapon for cutting through the clutter and making a lasting impression on your audience.

Know Your Audience:

The first step to creating engaging content is knowing your audience inside and out. What makes them tick? What are their interests, passions, and pain points? The better you understand your audience, the easier it'll be to create content that resonates with them on a deeper level.

Tell a Story:

At the heart of engaging content lies the art of storytelling because storytelling is a powerful tool that captures the attention of your audience, evokes emotions, and forges connections. Humans are naturally drawn to stories because they resonate with our experiences, beliefs, and emotions. When you tell a compelling story, you create a narrative that not only entertains but also engages and inspires your audience. Here's why storytelling is important, along with an example:

Reason:

1. **Captivating Attention:** Stories have the ability to capture the attention of your audience in a way that facts and figures alone cannot. When you tell a story, you create a sense of intrigue and curiosity that compels people to listen and pay attention to what you have to say.

2. **Eliciting Emotions:** Stories have the power to evoke emotions, whether it's joy, sadness, excitement, or empathy. When you tap into your audience's emotions, you create a deeper connection that resonates on a personal level and leaves a lasting impression.

3. **Forging Connections:** Stories create a sense of shared experience and connection between you and your audience. When you tell a story that your audience can relate to, you create a bond

that goes beyond a transactional relationship, fostering loyalty and trust.

Example:

Imagine you're a food blogger sharing a recipe for a classic family dish on your blog. Instead of simply listing the ingredients and instructions, you begin your post with a personal anecdote about how this recipe has been passed down through generations in your family. You share memories of cooking with your grandmother in her kitchen, the aromas that filled the air, and the joy of sharing meals with loved ones. As you weave this story throughout your post, you not only provide valuable information about the recipe but also create an emotional connection with your audience. Readers are drawn in by your personal story, and they feel inspired to recreate the dish in their own kitchens, knowing that it carries with it a sense of tradition and nostalgia.

In this example, storytelling enhances the content by adding depth, emotion, and relatability. By sharing a personal anecdote, the food blogger creates a narrative that resonates with readers on a deeper level, making the recipe more than just a list of ingredients – it becomes a shared experience that brings people together. This emotional connection not only makes the content more engaging but also encourages readers to take action, whether it's trying the recipe themselves or sharing it with others.

Spark Conversation:

Engaging content isn't just about grabbing attention – it's about sparking conversation and fostering community. Encourage your audience to share their thoughts, opinions, and experiences in the comments. Ask questions, run polls, and invite them to join the conversation. The more you engage with your audience, the more invested they'll become in your brand.

Quality Over Quantity:

When it comes to creating engaging content, remember: it's quality over quantity. Focus on creating content that adds value to your audience's lives – whether it's entertaining, educating, inspiring, or informing. Don't just churn out content for the sake of it – take the time to craft content that's meaningful and memorable.

Experiment and Iterate:

Finally, don't be afraid to experiment and iterate with your content. What works for one audience might not work for another, so it's important to stay agile and responsive. Test different types of content, formats, and messaging to see what resonates most with your audience, and don't be afraid to pivot if something isn't working.

The Bottom Line:

Creating engaging and share-worthy content is the key to capturing your audience's attention and building a loyal following on social media. By knowing your audience, telling compelling stories, sparking conversation, prioritizing quality over quantity, and experimenting and iterating with your content, you'll create a content strategy that keeps your audience coming back for more. So, roll up your sleeves, unleash your creativity, and let's craft some content that'll make waves in the digital world!

Finding Your Voice: Tips for Content Strategy and Brand Identity

Ready to unlock the secrets to crafting a content strategy that'll make your brand stand out from the crowd? Well, you're in luck because we're diving deep into the world of brand voice and identity, and how to develop a content strategy that's uniquely you.

Know Thyself:

Before you can start crafting content, you need to know who you are as a brand. What are your values, mission, and personality? What sets you apart from the competition? Take some time to define your brand identity – the essence of who you are and what you stand for.

Define Your Audience:

Next up, it's time to get to know your audience inside and out. Who are they? What are their interests, passions, and pain points? The better you understand your audience, the easier it'll be to create content that resonates with them on a deeper level.

Craft Your Brand Voice:

Your brand voice is the personality of your brand – it's how you communicate with your audience and the tone and style you use to express yourself. Are you playful and whimsical, or serious and authoritative? Whatever your brand voice, make sure it's authentic and consistent across all your content.

Set Clear Goals and Objectives:

Like any good strategy, your content strategy should have clear goals and objectives. What are you hoping to achieve with your content? Increased brand awareness? More leads? Higher engagement? By setting specific, measurable goals, you'll be able to track your progress and measure your success.

Choose the Right Platforms:

Not all social media platforms are created equal, and neither are all brands. Choose the platforms that align best with your brand identity and where your audience hangs out online.

Whether it's Instagram, Twitter, LinkedIn, or TikTok, focus your efforts on the platforms that offer the best opportunity to reach and engage with your target audience.

Plan Your Content Calendar:

Once you've defined your brand voice, audience, and goals, it's time to start planning your content calendar. Map out your content themes, topics, and posting schedule in advance, but leave room for flexibility and spontaneity. Your content calendar should be a guide, not a rigid rulebook.

Create Engaging Content:

Finally, it's time to start creating content that'll captivate your audience and keep them coming back for more. Whether it's blog posts, videos, infographics, or social media posts, focus on creating content that adds value to your audience's lives – whether it's entertaining, educating, inspiring, or informing.

The Bottom Line:

Developing a content strategy and establishing your brand voice and identity is the foundation of any successful social media strategy. By knowing who you are as a brand, understanding your audience, setting clear goals, choosing the right platforms, planning your content calendar, and creating engaging content, you'll build a content strategy that's uniquely you and sets you apart from the competition. So, grab your pen and paper, unleash your creativity, and let's craft a content strategy that'll make waves in the digital world!

Building Strong Foundations: Content Pillars and Themes

Are you ready to build a sturdy framework for your content

strategy? Well, you're in luck because we're diving deep into the world of content pillars and themes, and how to identify the ones that align perfectly with your business objectives.

What Are Content Pillars?

Think of content pillars as the sturdy columns that support the roof of your content strategy. They're the core topics or themes that your content revolves around and represent the key areas of expertise or interest for your brand. By defining your content pillars, you'll create a cohesive framework that ties all your content together and reinforces your brand identity.

Identify Your Business Objectives:

Before you can start brainstorming content pillars, you need to get clear on your business objectives. What are you hoping to achieve with your content? Increased brand awareness? More leads? Higher sales? By aligning your content pillars with your business objectives, you'll ensure that every piece of content you create serves a purpose and moves you closer to your goals.

Know Your Audience:

Next up, it's time to get inside the minds of your audience and understand what makes them tick. What are their interests, passions, and pain points? What questions are they asking, and what problems are they trying to solve? The better you understand your audience, the easier it'll be to identify content pillars that resonate with them on a deeper level.

Brainstorm Content Themes:

Once you've got a clear picture of your business objectives and audience, it's time to start brainstorming content themes that align with both. Think about the key topics or areas of expertise that are relevant to your brand and that your audience is interested in. These could be industry trends, product features, customer stories, or how-to guides – the sky's the limit!

Narrow it Down:

With your list of potential content themes in hand, it's time to narrow it down to the core pillars that will form the foundation of your content strategy. Look for themes that align closely with your brand identity, resonate with your audience, and support your business objectives. Aim for three to five content pillars to keep your strategy focused and manageable.

Create a Content Calendar:

Once you've identified your content pillars, it's time to start planning your content calendar. Map out your content themes, topics, and posting schedule in advance, making sure to balance variety and consistency. Your content calendar should reflect the diversity of your content pillars while staying true to your brand voice and identity.

Stay Flexible and Evolve:

Finally, remember that your content pillars aren't set in stone. As your business evolves and your audience's interests shift, you may need to adjust your content strategy accordingly. Stay flexible, keep an eye on emerging trends, and be willing to experiment and iterate with your content pillars to keep your strategy fresh and relevant.

The Bottom Line:

Identifying content pillars and themes that align with your business objectives is the key to building a strong and cohesive content strategy. By knowing your audience, defining your business objectives, brainstorming content themes, and creating a content calendar that reflects your content pillars, you'll create a framework that supports your brand identity and helps you achieve your goals. So, grab your hard hat and hammer, and let's start building!

Best Practices for Creating Engaging Content

Hello creative wizard! Ready to breathe life into your content and captivate your audience's attention? Well, you're in for a treat because we're diving into the world of content creation and sharing some best practices for crafting compelling text, captivating images, captivating videos, and interactive media that'll leave your audience craving more.

Text: Crafting Compelling Copy

Let's start with the written word – the bread and butter of content creation. When it comes to crafting text-based content, clarity is key. Keep your messaging clear, concise, and easy to understand, avoiding jargon or overly complex language. Use storytelling techniques to draw your audience in and evoke emotion, and don't forget to include a strong call to action to prompt them to take the next step.

Images: Painting a Picture

Next up, we've got images – the visual storytellers of the digital world. When creating images for your content, focus on quality over quantity. Choose high-resolution photos that are visually appealing and relevant to your brand and message. Use composition techniques like the rule of thirds and leading lines to create visually engaging images that draw the eye, and don't be afraid to experiment with filters, overlays, and text overlays to add depth and personality to your visuals.

Videos: Lights, Camera, Action!

Now, let's talk about everyone's favorite – videos! Video content has exploded in popularity in recent years, and for good reason – it's engaging, entertaining, and highly shareable. When creating video content, keep it short and sweet – attention spans are short on social media, so get to the point quickly. Use eye-catching visuals, captivating storytelling, and dynamic editing techniques to keep your audience hooked from start to finish, and don't forget to optimize your videos for mobile viewing.

Interactive Media: Engage and Delight

Last but not least, we've got interactive media – the new kid on the block in the world of content creation. Interactive media, such as quizzes, polls, and live streams, offers a unique opportunity to engage your audience in a two-way conversation and create immersive experiences that leave a lasting impression. When creating interactive content, focus on providing value and entertainment to your audience, and encourage them to participate actively in the experience. Whether it's polling your followers on their favorite products or hosting a live Q&A session, interactive media allows you to create memorable experiences that drive engagement and foster loyalty.

Experiment and Iterate:

No matter what type of content you're creating, remember to stay flexible and be willing to experiment and iterate with your content strategy. What works for one audience might not work for another, so don't be afraid to try new things and see what resonates most with your audience. And most importantly, have fun with it! Content creation is your chance to unleash your creativity and express your brand's unique personality, so don't be afraid to let your imagination run wild.

The Bottom Line:

Creating engaging content is the heart and soul of social media marketing. By following these best practices for crafting compelling text, captivating images, dynamic videos, and interactive media, you'll create content that captures your audience's attention, sparks conversation, and drives meaningful engagement. So, grab your camera, fire up your laptop, and let's get creative!

Chapter 3: Building and Growing Your Social Media Presence

Strategies for Optimizing Social Media Profiles

Ready to turn your social media profiles into shining beacons of visibility and engagement? Well, you're in luck because we're diving deep into the world of profile optimization and sharing some tried-and-true strategies to help you stand out from the crowd and make a lasting impression on your audience.

Choose the Right Profile Picture:

First impressions matter, and your profile picture is often the first thing people see when they stumble upon your profile. Choose a high-quality, professional-looking photo that accurately represents your brand and personality. Make sure your face or logo is clear and easily recognizable, even at smaller sizes.

Craft a Compelling Bio:

Your bio is your chance to make a memorable first impression and give visitors a glimpse into who you are and what you're all about. Keep it concise and to the point, highlighting key information such as your name, title, location, and a brief overview of what you do. Use keywords related to your industry or niche to improve discoverability, and don't forget to include a call to action to encourage visitors to take the next step, whether it's following you, visiting your website, or signing up for your newsletter.

Optimize Your Username and Handle:

Your username and handle are the digital fingerprints that identify you across social media. Choose a username and handle that are easy to remember, spell, and pronounce, and ideally, consistent across all your social media profiles. If your ideal username is already taken, consider adding a modifier such as your location or profession to differentiate yourself.

Complete Your Profile:

Don't leave any stone unturned when it comes to completing your profile. Fill out all the relevant fields, including your website URL, contact information, and links to other social media profiles. The more information you provide, the easier it'll be for visitors to learn more about you and engage with your content.

Use Keywords Strategically:

Keywords aren't just for search engines – they're also essential for optimizing your social media profiles for maximum visibility. Use relevant keywords related to your industry, niche, and target audience throughout your profile, including in your bio, headline, and posts. This will improve your profile's discoverability and make it easier for people to find you when searching for related topics.

Post Consistently and Engage with Your Audience:

Optimizing your social media profiles isn't just about setting it and forgetting it – it's an ongoing process that requires consistent effort and engagement. Post regularly to keep your audience engaged and informed, and don't be afraid to interact with your followers through comments, messages, and likes. The more you engage with your audience, the stronger your relationships will become, and the more likely they'll be to stick around and become loyal fans.

Track Your Performance and Adjust Your Strategy:

Finally, don't forget to track your profile's performance and adjust your strategy accordingly. Use analytics tools provided by the social media platforms to monitor key metrics such as follower growth, engagement rates, and post reach. Pay attention to what's working and what's not, and be willing to experiment and iterate with your strategy to optimize your profile for maximum visibility and engagement.

The Bottom Line:

Optimizing your social media profiles is the first step towards building a strong and successful presence on social media. By following these strategies for choosing the right profile picture, crafting a compelling bio, optimizing your username and handle, completing your profile, using keywords strategically, posting consistently, engaging with your audience, and tracking your performance, you'll create profiles that shine bright and attract attention from all the right people. So, polish up your profile, put your best foot forward, and let's make a splash on social media!

Tips for Increasing Followers and Building a Community

Spread your wings and grow your tribe! You're in for a treat because we're diving into the world of follower growth and sharing some tried-and-true tips to help you expand your reach and build a loyal community around your brand.

1. Know Your Audience Inside and Out:

Understanding your audience is the key to growing your follower count and building a loyal community. Take the time to get to know your audience's interests, preferences, and pain points, and tailor your content to resonate with them on a deeper level. The better you understand your audience, the more likely they'll be to follow you and engage with your content.

2. Post Consistently and Quality Content:

Consistency is key when it comes to growing your follower count. Post regularly to keep your audience engaged and informed, but don't sacrifice quality for quantity. Focus on creating content that adds value to your audience's lives – whether it's entertaining, educating, inspiring, or informing. The more value you provide, the more likely people will be to follow you and stick around.

3. Engage with Your Audience:

Building a loyal community isn't just about broadcasting your message – it's about fostering two-way communication and building meaningful relationships with your audience. Take the time to engage with your followers through comments, messages, and likes. Respond to their questions, acknowledge their feedback, and show them that you value their input. The more you engage with your audience, the more invested they'll become in your brand and the more likely they'll be to stick around.

4. Collaborate with Others:

Collaboration is a powerful way to expand your reach and connect with new audiences. Partner with influencers, brands, or organizations in your niche to cross-promote each other's content and introduce your brand to new followers. Look for opportunities to guest post on other people's blogs, participate in joint webinars or events, or collaborate on social media giveaways or challenges. The more you collaborate, the more exposure you'll get, and the more followers you'll attract.

5. Use Hashtags Strategically:

Hashtags are a powerful tool for increasing your visibility and reaching new audiences on social media. Research relevant hashtags related to your industry, niche, or target audience, and use them strategically in your posts to expand your reach. Experiment with different combinations of hashtags to see which ones resonate most with your audience and drive the most engagement. And don't forget to create your own branded hashtag to encourage user-generated content and foster a sense of community around your brand.

6. Run Contests and Giveaways:

Contests and giveaways are a fun and effective way to incentivize people to follow you and engage with your content. Whether it's a photo contest, a caption contest, or a random giveaway, offering a prize or incentive can motivate people to take action and follow you. Just make sure to follow the rules and guidelines of the platform you're using, and be transparent about the terms and conditions of the contest or giveaway.

7. Stay Authentic and Genuine:

Above all, authenticity is the secret sauce to building a loyal community around your brand. Be genuine, transparent, and true to your brand values in everything you do. Show your personality, share your story, and let your passion shine through in your content. People are drawn to authenticity, and the more genuine you are, the more likely they'll be to connect with you on a deeper level and become loyal followers.

The Bottom Line:

Growing your follower count and building a loyal community takes time, effort, and patience, but the rewards are well worth it. By knowing your audience, posting consistently and quality content, engaging with your audience, collaborating with others, using hashtags strategically, running contests and giveaways, and staying authentic and genuine, you'll create a tribe of loyal followers who are passionate about your brand and eager to spread the word. So, spread your wings, soar to new heights, and let's build a community that's as strong as it is loyal!

The Power of Collaboration

Become a collaborative genius! How to harness the power of user-generated content and influencer partnerships to take your brand to new heights? Well, you're in for an adventure because we're diving into the world of collaboration and sharing some insider tips on how to expand your reach through the magic of user-generated content and influencer partnerships.

User-Generated Content:

Let's start with user-generated content (UGC) – the unsung hero of social media marketing. UGC is any content created by your audience, whether it's photos, videos, reviews, or testimonials, that features your brand or products. Leveraging UGC allows you to tap into the creativity and authenticity of your audience and turn them into brand advocates and ambassadors.

Encourage and Reward:

The key to leveraging UGC is to encourage and reward your audience for creating and sharing content featuring your brand.

Whether it's through branded hashtags, contests, or incentives like discounts or giveaways, make it easy and fun for your audience to participate and share their experiences with your brand. The more you encourage and reward UGC, the more likely people will be to create and share content featuring your brand.

Curate and Showcase:

Once you've got a treasure trove of UGC at your disposal, it's time to curate and showcase it across your social media channels. Share user-generated photos, videos, reviews, and testimonials on your social media profiles, website, and marketing materials to add authenticity and credibility to your brand. Not only does this showcase your loyal customers and fans, but it also creates a sense of community around your brand and encourages others to join in the fun.

Influencer Partnerships:

Now, let's talk about influencer partnerships – the ultimate collaboration for expanding your reach and tapping into new audiences. Influencers are social media personalities or content creators with large, engaged followings who can help amplify your message and introduce your brand to new audiences. Partnering with influencers allows you to leverage their credibility, authority, and reach to connect with new customers and grow your brand.

Find the Right Fit:

When it comes to influencer partnerships, it's essential to find the right fit for your brand. Look for influencers whose values, audience, and aesthetic align with yours, and who have an engaged and authentic following. Consider factors like audience demographics, engagement rates, and past collaborations when choosing influencers to partner with. The more aligned an influencer is with your brand, the more authentic and effective the partnership will be.

Collaborate and Co-Create:

Once you've found the perfect influencer partner, it's time to collaborate and co-create content that resonates with their audience and yours. Work together to brainstorm ideas, create compelling content, and develop a strategy for sharing and promoting it across your respective channels. Whether it's sponsored posts, product reviews, or takeover campaigns, find creative ways to integrate your brand into the influencer's content in a way that feels authentic and organic.

Measure and Iterate:

As with any marketing strategy, it's essential to measure the success of your influencer partnerships and UGC campaigns and iterate based on the results. Track key metrics like reach, engagement, website traffic, and conversions to gauge the effectiveness of your collaborations and make adjustments as needed. Experiment with different types of influencers, content formats, and messaging to see what resonates most with your audience and drives the most significant results.

The Bottom Line:

Leveraging user-generated content and influencer partnerships is a powerful way to expand your reach, build credibility, and connect with new audiences. By encouraging and rewarding UGC, curating and showcasing it across your channels, finding the right influencers to partner with, collaborating and co-creating compelling content, and measuring and iterating based on the results, you'll harness the power of collaboration to take your brand to new heights. So, reach out, collaborate, and let's create some magic together!

Best Practices for Meaningful Interactions with Audience

Ready to turn your social media channels into vibrant communities buzzing with meaningful interactions? Well, you're in for a treat because we're diving into the world of engagement and sharing some best practices for fostering meaningful conversations with your audience.

1. Be Authentic and Genuine:

Authenticity is the name of the game when it comes to fostering meaningful interactions with your audience. Be genuine, transparent, and true to your brand values in everything you do. Show your personality, share your story, and let your passion shine through in your content and interactions. People are drawn to authenticity, and the more genuine you are, the more likely they'll be to engage with you on a deeper level.

Example: Imagine you're a small business owner sharing behind-the-scenes glimpses of your day-to-day operations on social media. Instead of just posting polished and perfect photos, you share the ups and downs, the successes and failures, and the real-life moments that make your brand unique. Your audience appreciates your honesty and authenticity and feels more connected to your brand as a result.

2. Ask Questions and Encourage Conversation:

One of the easiest ways to foster meaningful interactions with your audience is to ask questions and encourage conversation. Whether it's through polls, quizzes, or open-ended prompts, invite your audience to share their thoughts, opinions, and experiences. The more you engage with your audience and invite them to participate in the conversation, the stronger your relationships will become.

Example: Let's say you're a fitness influencer hosting a live Q&A session on Instagram. Instead of just answering questions from your audience, you actively encourage them to ask questions, share their own fitness journeys, and offer advice and support to one another. The result? A dynamic and engaging conversation that leaves everyone feeling motivated and inspired.

3. Respond Promptly and Thoughtfully:

When your audience takes the time to engage with your content or reach out to you directly, it's essential to respond promptly and thoughtfully. Whether it's through comments, messages, or mentions, make an effort to acknowledge and respond to every interaction, no matter how big or small. The more responsive and attentive you are, the more valued and appreciated your audience will feel.

Example: Imagine you're a beauty brand responding to comments on your latest Instagram post. Instead of just liking or ignoring comments from your followers, you take the time to respond to each one individually, thanking them for their support, answering their questions, and engaging in conversation. Your audience feels seen, heard, and appreciated, fostering a sense of loyalty and connection to your brand.

4. Create a Sense of Community:

Building a sense of community around your brand is essential for fostering meaningful interactions with your audience. Encourage your followers to connect with one another, share their experiences, and support one another in their journey. Whether it's through dedicated Facebook groups, Twitter chats, or Instagram hashtags, create spaces where your audience can come together to connect, collaborate, and celebrate.

Example: Let's say you're a wellness blogger hosting a weekly Twitter chat on #WellnessWednesday. Each week, you pose a new discussion topic related to health and wellness and invite your followers to join the conversation using the hashtag. Your audience shares their tips, struggles, and success stories, fostering a sense of camaraderie and support within the community.

5. Show Appreciation and Recognition:

Finally, don't forget to show appreciation and recognition to your audience for their engagement and support. Whether it's through shoutouts, reposts, or exclusive perks and rewards, acknowledge and celebrate your most loyal followers and contributors. The more you show your appreciation, the more motivated and inspired your audience will be to continue engaging with your brand.

Example: Imagine you're a fashion brand featuring user-generated content from your followers on your Instagram Stories. Each week, you highlight a different follower and their outfit of the day, tagging them and thanking them for their support. Your audience feels valued and appreciated, encouraging them to continue engaging with your brand and sharing their content.

The Bottom Line:

Fostering meaningful interactions with your audience is the key to building strong and lasting relationships that drive loyalty and advocacy for your brand. By being authentic and genuine, asking questions and encouraging conversation, responding promptly and thoughtfully, creating a sense of community, and showing appreciation and recognition, you'll create an engaged and invested audience that's eager to support and champion your brand. So, spark the conversation, build connections, and let's create a community that's as vibrant as it is meaningful!

Chapter 4:
Leveraging Social
Media Advertising
and Promotion

Ready to take your brand to the next level with social media advertising? Well, you're in for a treat because we're diving into the world of advertising options available on major social media platforms, and sharing everything you need to know to make the most of your advertising dollars.

1. Facebook Advertising:

Let's start with the big kahuna – Facebook advertising. With over 2.8 billion monthly active users, Facebook offers unparalleled reach and targeting options for advertisers. Whether you're looking to drive website traffic, generate leads, or boost sales, Facebook has an advertising solution for you. From sponsored posts and carousel ads to lead generation forms and dynamic ads, the possibilities are endless.

Example: Imagine you're a small e-commerce business looking to promote your latest product line on Facebook. You decide to run a series of carousel ads showcasing your products in action, with each image linking to a different product page on your website. By targeting your ads to users interested in similar products or brands, you're able to reach a highly relevant audience and drive traffic and sales to your website.

2. Instagram Advertising:

Next up, we've got Instagram – the visual powerhouse of the social media world. With over 1 billion monthly active users, Instagram offers advertisers a highly engaged and visually-driven platform to showcase their products and services. Whether you're looking to raise brand awareness, drive app installs, or increase engagement, Instagram has a variety of advertising options to suit your needs. From photo ads and video ads to Instagram Stories and IGTV ads, there's something for everyone on Instagram.

Example: Let's say you're a fashion brand looking to reach a younger, fashion-forward audience on Instagram. You decide to run a series of Instagram Stories ads featuring behind-the-scenes footage from your latest photo shoot, with a swipe-up link to shop the featured looks. By targeting your ads to users interested in fashion and lifestyle content, you're able to reach a highly engaged audience and drive traffic and sales to your website.

3. Twitter (X) Advertising:

Moving on to Twitter – the platform where conversations happen in real-time. With over 330 million monthly active users, Twitter offers advertisers a unique opportunity to join the conversation and reach a highly engaged audience. Whether you're looking to drive brand awareness, increase website traffic, or boost app installs, Twitter has a range of advertising options to help you achieve your goals. From promoted tweets and trends to Twitter Cards and video ads, there's no shortage of ways to get your message heard on Twitter.

Example: Imagine you're a tech startup looking to raise

awareness for your new app on Twitter. You decide to run a series of promoted tweets targeting users interested in technology and innovation, with a call-to-action to download your app. By leveraging Twitter's targeting options to reach users who are likely to be interested in your app, you're able to increase awareness and drive downloads among your target audience.

4. LinkedIn Advertising:

Last but not least, we've got LinkedIn – the professional networking platform. With over 700 million members, LinkedIn offers advertisers a unique opportunity to reach a highly targeted and affluent audience of professionals and decision-makers. Whether you're looking to generate leads, drive website traffic, or recruit top talent, LinkedIn has a range of advertising options to help you achieve your goals. From sponsored content and InMail to dynamic ads and LinkedIn Video ads, there's something for every B2B marketer on LinkedIn.

Example: Let's say you're a B2B software company looking to generate leads for your latest product on LinkedIn. You decide to run a series of sponsored content ads targeting users in specific industries and job roles, with a lead generation form prompting users to request a demo of your product. By targeting your ads to decision-makers and influencers in your target market, you're able to generate high-quality leads and drive sales for your business.

The Bottom Line:

Navigating the social media advertising landscape can feel overwhelming, but with the right strategy and know-how, you can make the most of your advertising dollars and achieve your marketing goals. By understanding the different advertising options available on major social media platforms like Facebook,

Instagram, Twitter, and LinkedIn, and leveraging them to reach your target audience with compelling and relevant messaging, you'll be well on your way to success. So, roll up your sleeves, fire up your ads manager, and let's make some magic happen!

Tips for Targeting Specific Demographics and Objectives

Ready to craft ad campaigns that hit the bullseye every time? Well, you're in for a treat because we're diving into the world of targeted advertising and sharing some insider tips on how to create effective ad campaigns that reach specific demographics and objectives.

1. Know Your Audience Inside and Out:

The key to creating effective ad campaigns is understanding your audience inside and out. Take the time to research and analyze your target demographics, including their age, gender, location, interests, and behaviors. The more you know about your audience, the better you'll be able to tailor your messaging and targeting to resonate with them on a deeper level.

Example: Imagine you're a travel agency looking to promote your latest vacation package to families with young children. You know that your target audience is likely to be parents aged 25-45 who live in urban areas and have an interest in family-friendly travel destinations. By targeting your ad campaign specifically to this demographic, you'll increase the likelihood of reaching people who are most likely to be interested in your offer.

2. Set Clear Objectives and KPIs:

Before you launch your ad campaign, it's essential to set clear objectives and key performance indicators (KPIs) to measure success. Whether you're looking to drive website traffic, generate leads, or increase sales, having clearly defined goals will help you focus your efforts and track your progress over time.

Example: Let's say you're a fitness brand looking to promote your new online workout program. Your primary objective is to drive sign-ups for your program, so you set a goal of generating 500 new leads within the next month. You also set KPIs to track metrics like click-through rate, conversion rate, and cost per lead to gauge the effectiveness of your ad campaign.

3. Tailor Your Messaging and Creative:

Once you know who you're targeting and what you're trying to achieve, it's time to tailor your messaging and creative to resonate with your audience. Use language, imagery, and offers that speak directly to your target demographics and address their pain points and desires. The more personalized and relevant your ads are, the more likely they'll be to capture your audience's attention and drive action.

Example: Imagine you're a beauty brand launching a new skincare product targeted towards millennials. You know that your target audience is interested in natural and eco-friendly products, so you highlight the product's organic ingredients and sustainable packaging in your ad creative. You also use language and imagery that reflects the youthful and trendy aesthetic of your target audience to capture their attention and drive engagement.

4. Test and Iterate:

Once your ad campaign is live, don't just set it and forget it – be sure to test and iterate to optimize performance over time. Experiment with different ad formats, targeting options, and messaging variations to see what resonates most with your audience.

Analyze the results and make adjustments as needed to improve your campaign's effectiveness and ROI.

Example: Let's say you're an e-commerce retailer running a Facebook ad campaign to promote your summer sale. You start by testing different ad creatives, headlines, and calls-to-action to see which combination drives the highest engagement and conversion rates. Based on the results, you optimize your campaign by reallocating budget towards the top-performing ads and pausing underperforming ones, ultimately increasing your ROI and driving more sales.

5. Monitor and Measure Results:

Finally, be sure to monitor and measure the results of your ad campaign regularly to track progress towards your objectives and identify areas for improvement. Use analytics tools provided by the advertising platform to track key metrics like impressions, clicks, conversions, and return on investment (ROI). Use these insights to inform future campaigns and make data-driven decisions to maximize your advertising effectiveness.

Example: Imagine you're a small business owner running a Google Ads campaign to drive traffic to your website. You regularly monitor your campaign's performance using the Google Ads dashboard, tracking metrics like click-through rate, cost per click, and conversion rate. You notice that one of your ad groups is underperforming compared to the others, so you reallocate budget towards the top-performing ad groups and adjust your targeting and messaging to improve results.

The Bottom Line:

Creating effective ad campaigns that target specific demographics and objectives is a blend of art and science. By knowing your audience, setting clear objectives, tailoring your messaging and creative, testing and iterating, and monitoring and measuring results, you'll be well on your way to crafting ad campaigns that hit the mark every time. So, roll up your sleeves, get creative, and let's make some magic happen!

Mastering Ad Budgeting, Monitoring, and Optimization

Interested in taking your ad campaigns to the next level by mastering the art of budgeting, monitoring, and optimization? Well, you're in for a treat because we're diving into the world of ad budgeting and sharing some insider tips on how to set budgets, monitor campaign performance, and optimize your ad creative and targeting for maximum results.

1. Setting Ad Budgets:

The first step in creating successful ad campaigns is setting realistic ad budgets that align with your objectives and resources. When determining your ad budget, consider factors such as your overall marketing goals, target audience size, competition, and expected return on investment (ROI). Whether you're working with a modest budget or a substantial investment, setting clear budgetary guidelines will help you make informed decisions and maximize your advertising effectiveness.

Example: Let's say you're a small business owner looking to promote your new product launch on Facebook. After analyzing your marketing goals and audience size, you decide to allocate $500 towards your Facebook ad campaign for the month. This budget allows you to reach a substantial portion of your target audience without breaking the bank, ensuring a healthy return on investment for your advertising dollars.

2. Monitoring Campaign Performance:

Once your ad campaign is live, it's essential to monitor performance regularly to track progress towards your objectives and identify areas for improvement. Use analytics tools provided by the advertising platform to track key metrics such as impressions, clicks, conversions, and return on ad spend (ROAS). Monitor performance trends over time and be on the lookout for any anomalies or unexpected changes that may require attention.

Example: Imagine you're running a Google Ads campaign to drive traffic to your e-commerce website. You regularly monitor your campaign's performance using the Google Ads dashboard, tracking metrics such as click-through rate (CTR), cost per click (CPC), and conversion rate. After a few weeks, you notice that your CPC has increased significantly, while your conversion rate has decreased. This indicates that your campaign may be under-performing, prompting you to investigate further and make adjustments as needed.

3. Optimizing Ad Creative and Targeting:

As you monitor your ad campaign performance, be sure to optimize your ad creative and targeting to improve results over time. Experiment with different ad formats, messaging variations, and targeting options to see what resonates most with your audience. Analyze the results and make adjustments as needed to optimize your campaign for maximum effectiveness and return on investment.

Example: Let's say you're a fashion retailer running Instagram ads to promote your summer collection. After analyzing campaign performance, you notice that ads featuring lifestyle imagery perform better than product-focused ads. You decide to shift your ad creative strategy to focus more on lifestyle content, highlighting the experiences and emotions associated with your brand. As a result, you see an increase in engagement and conversion rates, ultimately driving more sales for your business.

4. Scaling and Adjusting Budgets:

As your ad campaigns mature and performance improves, consider scaling and adjusting your budgets accordingly. If a campaign is performing well and delivering a healthy return on investment, consider allocating additional budget to further expand reach and drive more conversions. Conversely, if a campaign is underperforming or reaching diminishing returns, consider reallocating budget towards higher-performing campaigns or experimenting with different strategies to improve results.

Example: Imagine you're a software company running LinkedIn ads to generate leads for your latest product. After a few weeks, you notice that one of your ad campaigns is performing exceptionally well, driving a high volume of leads at a low cost per acquisition (CPA). In response, you decide to increase the budget for this campaign to further capitalize on its success and maximize lead generation efforts.

5. Continuous Learning and Improvement:

Finally, remember that advertising is an iterative process, and continuous learning and improvement are essential for long-term success. Stay up-to-date on industry trends and best practices, and be willing to experiment and iterate with your ad campaigns to find what works best for your brand and audience. By staying agile and adaptable, you'll be better equipped to navigate the ever-evolving landscape of digital advertising and drive meaningful results for your business.

Example: Let's say you're a marketing manager for a SaaS company running Facebook ads to promote your latest software update. After analyzing campaign performance, you notice that video ads outperform image ads in terms of engagement and conversion rates. In response, you decide to shift your ad creative strategy to focus more on video content, investing more budget towards video ads and experimenting with different storytelling techniques to capture your audience's attention.

The Bottom Line:

Mastering the art of ad budgeting, monitoring, and optimization is essential for creating successful ad campaigns that drive meaningful results for your business. By setting clear budgets, monitoring performance, optimizing ad creative and targeting, scaling and adjusting budgets, and continuously learning and improving, you'll be well on your way to maximizing your advertising effectiveness and achieving your marketing objectives. So, roll up your sleeves, dive into your ad campaigns, and let's make some magic happen!

Synergy: Integrating Paid Advertising with Organic Content

Hey there, synergy seeker! Unlock the full potential of your marketing efforts by integrating paid advertising with organic content! You're in for a treat because we're diving into the world of integrated marketing and sharing some best practices for combining paid advertising and organic content to maximize results.

1. Align Your Messaging and Branding:

The first step in integrating paid advertising with organic content is to ensure alignment across your messaging and branding. Your paid ads and organic content should share a consistent tone, voice, and visual style to create a cohesive brand experience for your audience. Whether you're promoting a new product launch or sharing behind-the-scenes glimpses of your brand, consistency is key to building trust and recognition with your audience.

Example: Imagine you're a lifestyle brand launching a new line of eco-friendly products. Your paid ads feature vibrant imagery and catchy taglines highlighting the sustainability and quality of your products. To complement your paid advertising efforts, you create organic content for your social media channels showcasing the production process, introducing the artisans behind the products, and sharing tips for living a more eco-conscious lifestyle. By aligning your messaging and branding across paid and organic channels, you create a seamless brand experience that resonates with your audience and drives engagement.

2. Leverage Paid Advertising to Amplify Organic Reach:

Paid advertising offers a powerful opportunity to amplify the reach of your organic content and ensure it reaches a wider audience. Use paid ads to promote your top-performing organic posts, blog articles, or videos to extend their reach beyond your existing followers and attract new audiences. By strategically boosting your organic content with paid advertising, you can increase visibility, engagement, and conversion opportunities for your brand.

Example: Let's say you're a food blogger who recently published a blog post featuring a collection of healthy recipes. The post performs exceptionally well organically, driving high levels of engagement and shares among your followers. To capitalize on its success and reach a broader audience, you decide to create a Facebook ad campaign promoting the blog post to users interested in healthy eating and cooking. By targeting your ad to a relevant audience and leveraging paid advertising to amplify your organic reach, you increase traffic to your blog and attract new readers interested in your content.

3. Use Organic Insights to Inform Paid Advertising Strategy:

Your organic content provides valuable insights into what resonates with your audience and what drives engagement and conversion. Use these insights to inform your paid advertising strategy and identify opportunities for targeting, messaging, and creative optimization. Analyze the performance of your top-performing organic content and use this data to refine your paid advertising efforts and maximize results.

Example: Imagine you're a fashion brand running a Facebook ad campaign to promote your latest collection. After analyzing the performance of your organic content on Instagram, you notice that posts featuring user-generated content showcasing customers wearing your products receive the highest engagement and conversion rates. In response, you decide to incorporate user-generated content into your paid ads, leveraging the authenticity and social proof to attract new customers and drive sales.

4. Create Seamless Cross-Promotion Opportunities:

Integrating paid advertising with organic content offers endless opportunities for cross-promotion and collaboration. Use your organic channels to tease upcoming paid campaigns, encourage engagement with your ads, and drive traffic to your website or landing pages. Similarly, use your paid ads to promote your organic content, encourage followership on your social media channels, and foster deeper connections with your audience.

Example: Let's say you're a travel influencer planning a sponsored Instagram campaign with a tourism board to promote a destination. Before launching the paid campaign, you create organic content on your blog and social media channels sharing travel tips, destination highlights, and behind-the-scenes glimpses of your trip preparation. As the paid campaign goes live, you leverage your organic channels to promote the sponsored content, driving traffic to the tourism board's website and increasing engagement with the campaign.

5. Measure and Iterate for Continuous Improvement:

As with any marketing strategy, it's essential to measure the performance of your integrated paid and organic efforts and iterate based on the results. Track key metrics such as reach, engagement, click-through rates, and conversion rates to gauge the effectiveness of your campaigns and identify areas for improvement. Use these insights to refine your strategy, optimize your messaging and targeting, and drive better results over time.

Example: Imagine you're a digital marketer running a LinkedIn ad campaign to promote a series of webinars on marketing best practices. As the campaign progresses, you closely monitor performance metrics such as click-through rates and webinar registrations. You notice that ads featuring compelling headlines and clear calls-to-action drive the highest engagement and conversion rates. Armed with this insight, you adjust your ad creative and messaging to align more closely with what resonates with your audience, resulting in improved campaign performance and higher webinar attendance.

The Bottom Line:

Integrating paid advertising with organic content offers a powerful opportunity to maximize the impact of your marketing efforts and drive meaningful results for your brand. By aligning your messaging and branding, leveraging paid advertising to amplify organic reach, using organic insights to inform paid advertising strategy, creating seamless cross-promotion opportunities, and measuring and iterating for continuous improvement, you'll create a cohesive and effective marketing strategy that resonates with your audience and drives engagement and conversion. So, embrace the power of synergy, blend your paid and organic efforts, and let's make some magic happen!

Chapter 5: Engaging and Retaining Your Audience

Strategies for Audience Engagement

Calling all engagement enthusiast! Ready to keep your audience coming back for more with consistent and compelling content? Well, you're in luck because we're diving into the world of audience engagement and sharing some tried-and-true strategies for maintaining consistent engagement with your audience and keeping them hooked on your brand.

1. Know Your Audience Inside and Out:

The foundation of consistent audience engagement is understanding your audience inside and out. Take the time to research and analyze your audience demographics, interests, preferences, and behaviors to tailor your content to their needs and preferences. The better you know your audience, the more effectively you can create content that resonates with them and keeps them coming back for more.

Example: Imagine you're a beauty brand targeting millennial women interested in skincare and makeup. Through audience research and analysis, you discover that your audience is passionate about clean beauty and sustainability. Armed with this insight, you create content focused on natural ingredients, eco-friendly packaging, and ethical sourcing practices, resonating with your audience's values and preferences and keeping them engaged with your brand.

2. Be Consistent and Reliable:

Consistency is key when it comes to maintaining audience engagement. Establish a regular posting schedule and stick to it, whether it's daily, weekly, or monthly. Consistent posting helps build anticipation and expectation among your audience, keeping them coming back for more and establishing your brand as a reliable source of valuable content.

Example: Let's say you're a fitness influencer posting workout videos on YouTube. You commit to posting a new workout video every Monday, Wednesday, and Friday at 9 a.m. By sticking to your posting schedule, you create a sense of routine and reliability among your audience, encouraging them to return to your channel regularly for their dose of fitness inspiration and motivation.

3. Spark Conversations and Encourage Participation:

Engagement is a two-way street, so be sure to spark conversations and encourage participation from your audience. Ask questions, pose polls, and invite your audience to share their thoughts, opinions, and experiences in the comments. The more you engage with your audience and invite them to participate in the conversation, the more invested they'll become in your brand.

Example: Imagine you're a food blogger sharing a recipe on Instagram. In your caption, you ask your audience to share their favorite ingredient substitutions or cooking hacks in the comments. Your audience responds enthusiastically, sharing their own tips and tricks and sparking a lively conversation around the recipe. By actively engaging with your audience and inviting them to participate, you create a sense of community and connection that keeps them coming back for more.

4. Offer Value and Utility:

To maintain consistent engagement with your audience, focus on offering value and utility in your content. Whether it's educational, entertaining, or inspirational, your content should provide something of value to your audience and enhance their lives in some way. By consistently delivering content that meets your audience's needs and interests, you'll establish yourself as a trusted source of information and keep them coming back for more.

Example: Let's say you're a personal finance blogger sharing budgeting tips on your website. You create a series of blog posts and videos offering practical advice on saving money, managing debt, and building wealth. Your audience finds your content informative and actionable, implementing your tips and strategies into their own financial lives. As a result, they continue to return to your blog for more valuable insights and recommendations.

5. Be Authentic and Genuine:

Last but not least, authenticity is essential for maintaining consistent engagement with your audience. Be genuine, transparent, and true to your brand values in everything you do. Share your story, show your personality, and let your passion shine through in your content and interactions. Authenticity builds trust and connection with your audience, keeping them engaged and loyal to your brand over the long term.

Example: Imagine you're a travel influencer sharing your adventures on social media. Instead of just posting picture-perfect travel photos, you share the ups and downs, the highs and lows, and the real-life moments that make your travels unique. Your audience appreciates your honesty and authenticity, feeling like they're right there with you on your journey. As a result, they continue to follow along and engage with your content, eager to see where your next adventure takes you.

The Bottom Line:

Maintaining consistent engagement with your audience is essential for building lasting relationships and driving loyalty and advocacy for your brand. By knowing your audience inside and out, being consistent and reliable, sparking conversations and encouraging participation, offering value and utility, and being authentic and genuine, you'll keep your audience coming back for more and create a community that's as engaged as it is loyal. So, keep the conversation going, nurture those relationships, and let's create some magic together!

Tips for Tracking Engagement and Gathering Audience Insights

Ready to unlock the secrets hidden within your social media analytics and gain valuable insights into your audience's behavior and preferences? Well, you're in luck because we're diving into the world of social media analytics and sharing some insider tips on how to track engagement metrics and gather audience insights like a pro.

1. Define Your Key Engagement Metrics:

The first step in leveraging social media analytics is to define your key engagement metrics – the data points that matter most to your business goals. Whether it's likes, comments, shares, clicks, or conversions, identify the metrics that align with your objectives and provide meaningful insights into your audience's behavior and interactions with your content.

Example: Imagine you're a fashion brand looking to increase brand awareness on Instagram. Your key engagement metrics might include likes, comments, and shares on your posts, as well as click-through rates on your website links. By tracking these metrics over time, you can gauge the effectiveness of your content and identify opportunities for improvement to drive greater engagement and reach.

2. Use Built-In Analytics Tools:

Most social media platforms offer built-in analytics tools that provide valuable insights into your audience's behavior and engagement with your content. Take advantage of these tools to track key metrics, analyze performance trends, and gain a deeper understanding of what resonates with your audience. Whether it's Facebook Insights, Instagram Insights, or Twitter Analytics, these tools provide a wealth of data to inform your strategy and decision-making.

Example: Let's say you're a food blogger using Instagram to share recipes and cooking tips. You regularly check your Instagram Insights dashboard to track metrics such as reach, impressions, engagement, and follower demographics. You notice that posts featuring step-by-step cooking tutorials receive the highest engagement and shares among your audience. Armed with this insight, you double down on creating more tutorial-style content to drive greater engagement and reach on your Instagram profile.

3. Monitor Performance Trends Over Time:

As you track engagement metrics and gather audience insights, be sure to monitor performance trends over time to identify patterns and opportunities for optimization. Look for trends in engagement, reach, and conversion rates, and analyze how changes in your content, posting frequency, or targeting strategies impact performance. By staying vigilant and monitoring performance trends, you can adapt and iterate your strategy to maximize results.

Example: Imagine you're a travel influencer running Facebook ads to promote your latest travel guidebook. After a few weeks, you notice that ad engagement and click-through rates are declining, despite consistent ad spend. Upon further analysis, you discover that ad fatigue may be setting in among your audience, prompting you to refresh your ad creative and messaging to reignite interest and engagement. By monitoring performance trends over time, you can proactively address issues and optimize your campaigns for better results.

4. Dive Deep into Audience Demographics:

In addition to tracking engagement metrics, social media analytics also provide valuable insights into your audience demographics – who they are, where they're from, and what they're interested in. Use this demographic data to better understand your audience's preferences and tailor your content and targeting strategies to their needs and interests.

Example: Let's say you're a fitness influencer using Twitter to share workout tips and motivational quotes. You analyze your Twitter Analytics dashboard and discover that the majority of your followers are young adults aged 18-34 who are interested in health and fitness. Armed with this demographic insight, you create content that speaks directly to your audience's interests and goals, such as workout routines, healthy recipes, and inspirational success stories. By tailoring your content to your audience demographics, you increase engagement and build a stronger connection with your followers.

5. Experiment and Iterate Based on Insights:

Finally, don't be afraid to experiment and iterate based on the insights gathered from your social media analytics. Test different content formats, posting times, and targeting strategies to see what resonates most with your audience and drives the highest engagement and conversion rates. Use A/B testing and experimentation to refine your approach over time and optimize your social media strategy for maximum effectiveness.

Example: Imagine you're a digital marketer running LinkedIn ads to promote a series of webinars on marketing best practices. After analyzing ad performance, you notice that ads featuring video content outperform static image ads in terms of engagement and conversion rates. In response, you shift your ad creative strategy to focus more on video content, reallocating budget towards video ads and experimenting with different storytelling techniques to capture your audience's attention. By testing and iterating based on insights gathered from social media analytics, you optimize your ad campaigns for better results.

The Bottom Line:

Leveraging social media analytics is essential for tracking engagement metrics, gathering audience insights, and optimizing your social media strategy for success. By defining your key engagement metrics, using built-in analytics tools, monitoring performance trends over time, diving deep into audience demographics, and experimenting and iterating based on insights, you'll gain a deeper understanding of your audience and drive greater engagement and results for your business. So, roll up your sleeves, dive into your social media analytics, and let's uncover some insights together!

A Guide to Implementing Engagement Tactics

Kick your social media strategy up a notch by implementing some fun and interactive engagement tactics! We're diving into the world of engagement tactics and sharing some insider tips on how to spark interaction with your audience using contests, polls, and live streaming.

1. Host Engaging Contests and Giveaways:

Contests and giveaways are a fantastic way to spark interaction with your audience and generate excitement around your brand. Whether it's a photo contest, caption contest, or sweepstakes, hosting a contest encourages your audience to participate and engage with your content for a chance to win prizes. Be sure to promote your contest across all your social media channels and provide clear instructions on how to enter and win.

Example: Imagine you're a beauty brand launching a new product line. To generate buzz and excitement around the launch, you host a giveaway on Instagram where followers can enter to win a free bundle of products by tagging a friend and sharing their favorite makeup look using your hashtag. The contest garners hundreds of entries and sparks lively conversations among your audience, driving engagement and brand awareness.

2. Poll Your Audience for Feedback and Insights:

Polls are a great way to solicit feedback from your audience and gather insights into their preferences and opinions. Use polls to ask questions, gather feedback on new products or services, or simply spark conversation around trending topics. Polls are quick and easy for your audience to participate in, making them an effective way to engage with your audience and encourage interaction.

Example: Let's say you're a food blogger looking to crowdsource recipe ideas for your next blog post. You create a poll on Twitter asking your followers to vote for their favorite type of cuisine – Italian, Mexican, or Asian. The poll receives a high response rate, with your followers eagerly sharing their preferences and suggestions in the comments. Armed with this valuable feedback, you create a mouthwatering Italian pasta recipe for your next blog post, delighting your audience and fostering a sense of community.

3. Go Live with Interactive Streaming Sessions:

Live streaming is a powerful engagement tactic that allows you to connect with your audience in real-time and foster authentic interactions. Host live Q&A sessions, behind-the-scenes tours, product demonstrations, or interactive workshops to engage with your audience and provide value in a more personal and immersive way. Be sure to promote your live streams in advance and encourage your audience to tune in and participate.

Example: Imagine you're a fitness influencer hosting a live workout session on Facebook. You announce the live stream in advance on your social media channels and encourage your followers to join you for a high-energy cardio workout. During the live stream, you interact with your audience in real-time, answering questions, providing motivation, and offering personalized coaching tips. Your followers feel like they're working out alongside you, fostering a sense of camaraderie and community that keeps them coming back for more.

4. Encourage User-Generated Content and Collabora-

tion:

User-generated content (UGC) is a powerful engagement tactic that empowers your audience to become creators and collaborators. Encourage your audience to share their own content, stories, and experiences related to your brand or industry, and showcase their contributions on your social media channels. UGC not only fosters a sense of community and connection but also provides valuable social proof and authenticity for your brand.

Example: Let's say you're a travel brand hosting a photo contest on Instagram. You invite your followers to share their best travel photos using your branded hashtag for a chance to be featured on your profile. The contest generates a flood of stunning travel photos from around the world, showcasing the beauty and diversity of your audience's travel experiences. By sharing UGC on your profile, you not only engage with your audience but also inspire others to join in the conversation and share their own travel adventures.

5. Create Interactive Quizzes and Challenges:

Quizzes and challenges are fun and interactive ways to engage with your audience and spark friendly competition. Create quizzes related to your industry or niche, such as personality quizzes, trivia quizzes, or product quizzes, and encourage your audience to participate and share their results. Similarly, challenge your audience to complete tasks or activities related to your brand or content, and reward them for their participation.

Example: Imagine you're a wellness coach creating a fitness challenge on TikTok. You challenge your followers to complete a series of daily workouts and share their progress using your branded hashtag. Each day, you post a new workout video demonstrating the exercises and encouraging your audience to join in the challenge. The challenge gains momentum as more and more people participate, fostering a sense of community and accountability among your followers.

The Bottom Line:

Implementing engagement tactics such as contests, polls, live streaming, user-generated content, quizzes, and challenges is a fun and effective way to spark interaction with your audience and foster a sense of community and connection. By getting creative and experimenting with different engagement tactics, you'll not only increase engagement and brand awareness but also build lasting relationships with your audience that keep them coming back for more. So, get ready to ignite the conversation, inspire action, and let's create some magic together!

The Art of Authentic Engagement: Best Practices for Responding

Want to be a social butterfly! Ready to take your engagement game to the next level by mastering the art of responding to comments, messages, and feedback? Well, you're in luck because we're diving into the world of authentic engagement and sharing some best practices for responding to your audience in a timely and genuine manner.

1. Be Prompt and Proactive:

The first rule of engagement is to be prompt and proactive in your responses. When someone leaves a comment, sends a message, or provides feedback, acknowledge their input as soon as possible. Even if you can't provide a detailed response right away, a quick acknowledgment shows that you value their input and are actively listening to their needs and concerns.

Example: Imagine you're a small business owner managing your company's Facebook page. A customer leaves a comment on your latest post asking about product availability. Instead of waiting hours or days to respond, you reply to the comment within minutes, thanking the customer for their inquiry and providing information about product availability and pricing. Your prompt response not only addresses the customer's question but also demonstrates your commitment to excellent customer service.

2. Personalize Your Responses:

When responding to comments, messages, and feedback, take the time to personalize your responses whenever possible. Use the person's name, reference their specific question or comment, and tailor your response to their individual needs and concerns. Personalization shows that you're attentive to your audience and care about providing a meaningful and relevant experience for each person.

Example: Let's say you're a lifestyle blogger responding to comments on your Instagram post. Instead of using generic responses like "Thanks for your comment!" or "Glad you liked it!", you take the time to personalize your responses for each commenter. If someone asks about the brand of clothing you're wearing in a photo, you reply with the brand name and a link to the product page. If someone compliments your recipe and asks for cooking tips, you respond with personalized cooking advice and a friendly thank you. Your personalized responses not only engage with your audience but also foster a deeper connection and sense of camaraderie.

3. Show Genuine Appreciation and Gratitude:

Expressing genuine appreciation and gratitude is key to building strong relationships with your audience. When someone takes the time to leave a positive comment, share your content, or provide feedback, be sure to thank them sincerely for their support. Even a simple "thank you" goes a long way in making your audience feel valued and appreciated.

Example: Imagine you're a content creator on YouTube receiving positive feedback on your latest video. Instead of just liking the comments or giving generic responses, you take the time to reply to each commenter individually with a heartfelt thank you. You express your gratitude for their kind words and support, letting them know how much their feedback means to you and how it motivates you to create more content. Your genuine appreciation strengthens the bond with your audience and encourages continued engagement and support.

4. Address Concerns and Feedback with Empathy:

Not all comments and messages will be positive, and that's okay. When responding to negative feedback or addressing concerns, approach the situation with empathy and understanding. Listen actively to the person's concerns, acknowledge their feelings, and offer a solution or resolution to the best of your ability. Showing empathy demonstrates that you care about your audience's experience and are committed to addressing their needs and concerns.

Example: Let's say you're a customer service representative managing your company's Twitter account. A customer tweets about a negative experience they had with your product, expressing frustration and disappointment. Instead of ignoring the tweet or dismissing the customer's concerns, you reply to the tweet with a sincere apology and an offer to resolve the issue. You ask the customer to send you a direct message with more details so you can address their concerns promptly and effectively. Your empathetic response shows that you value the customer's feedback and are committed to providing a positive experience.

5. Foster Meaningful Conversations and Connections:

Finally, use your responses to comments, messages, and feedback as an opportunity to foster meaningful conversations and connections with your audience. Ask questions, solicit feedback, and encourage dialogue to deepen engagement and build a sense of community around your brand. The more you engage with your audience authentically, the stronger your relationships will become.

Example: Imagine you're a lifestyle influencer hosting a Q&A session on your Instagram Stories. You encourage your followers to submit questions via the question sticker and respond to each question with thoughtful and detailed answers. As the session progresses, you engage with your audience in real-time, answering follow-up questions, sharing personal anecdotes, and fostering genuine connections. Your Q&A session sparks meaningful conversations and strengthens the bond with your audience, leaving them feeling valued and heard.

The Bottom Line:

Responding to comments, messages, and feedback in a timely and authentic manner is essential for building strong relationships and fostering engagement with your audience. By being prompt and proactive, personalizing your responses, showing genuine appreciation and gratitude, addressing concerns with empathy, and fostering meaningful conversations and connections, you'll create a positive and engaging experience that keeps your audience coming back for more. So, roll up your sleeves, dive into those comments and messages, and let's start building some meaningful connections together!

Chapter 6: Measuring and Optimizing Your Social Media Strategy

Measuring Social Media Success

Hey there, metrics maven! Ready to dive into the world of tracking key performance indicators (KPIs) and measuring the success of your social media efforts? Well, you're in for a treat because we're about to uncover the power of metrics and show you how to evaluate the effectiveness of your social media strategy like a pro.

1. Understanding the Importance of KPIs:

First things first, let's talk about why tracking KPIs is so important. KPIs are like your compass in the vast ocean of social media. They provide direction, clarity, and insight into how well your social media efforts are performing and whether you're on track to achieve your business goals. By defining and tracking KPIs, you can measure progress, identify areas for improvement, and make informed decisions to optimize your strategy.

2. Defining Your Social Media KPIs:

The next step is to define your social media KPIs – the specific metrics that align with your business objectives and indicate success. KPIs can vary depending on your goals, but common examples include engagement metrics (likes, comments, shares), reach metrics (impressions, reach), conversion metrics (click-through rates, conversion rates), and brand awareness metrics (follower growth, mentions).

3. Measuring Engagement Metrics:

Let's start by looking at engagement metrics, which measure how actively your audience is interacting with your content. For example, you might track the number of likes, comments, shares, and mentions your posts receive on social media platforms. By measuring engagement metrics, you can gauge the level of interest and interaction with your content and identify which posts resonate most with your audience.

Detailed Example: Imagine you're a fashion brand running a social media campaign to promote your latest collection. You track engagement metrics such as likes, comments, and shares on your Instagram posts. After analyzing the data, you discover that posts featuring user-generated content (UGC) showcasing customers wearing your products receive significantly higher engagement than product photos alone. Armed with this insight, you shift your content strategy to focus more on UGC and encourage your audience to share their own photos, resulting in increased engagement and brand loyalty.

4. Evaluating Reach and Impressions:

Next up, let's talk about reach and impressions, which measure the visibility and exposure of your content on social media. Reach refers to the total number of unique users who have seen your content, while impressions represent the total number of times your content has been displayed. By measuring reach and impressions, you can assess the overall reach and impact of your social media efforts and identify opportunities to expand your audience.

Detailed Example: Continuing with the fashion brand example, you track reach and impressions on your Facebook ads promoting your latest collection. After analyzing the data, you notice that the ads targeting a younger demographic (ages 18-24) have a higher reach and lower cost-per-impression compared to ads targeting an older demographic (ages 35-44). Based on this insight, you allocate more budget towards targeting the younger demographic, resulting in increased reach and engagement with your target audience.

5. Monitoring Conversion Metrics:

Conversion metrics are perhaps the most critical KPIs for measuring the effectiveness of your social media efforts in driving desired actions or outcomes. Whether it's clicks, sign-ups, purchases, or downloads, conversion metrics indicate the extent to which your social media activities are contributing to your business objectives and generating tangible results.

Detailed Example: Let's say you're a software company running LinkedIn ads to promote your new productivity tool. You track conversion metrics such as click-through rates (CTR) and sign-ups for a free trial of your software. After analyzing the data, you discover that ads featuring customer testimonials and case studies have a significantly higher CTR and conversion rate compared to ads highlighting product features alone. Armed with this insight, you optimize your ad creative to focus more on customer stories and success stories, resulting in increased sign-ups and conversions.

6. Assessing Brand Awareness Metrics:

Last but not least, brand awareness metrics measure the visibility and recognition of your brand among your target audience. This can include metrics such as follower growth, mentions, and sentiment analysis. By monitoring brand awareness metrics, you can track the growth and perception of your brand over time and identify opportunities to strengthen your brand presence.

Detailed Example: Imagine you're a startup launching a new skincare brand on Instagram. You track brand awareness metrics such as follower growth, mentions, and sentiment analysis to assess the impact of your social media efforts on brand perception. After analyzing the data, you notice a steady increase in follower growth and positive sentiment towards your brand, indicating growing awareness and favorability among your target audience. Encouraged by these results, you continue to invest in building your brand presence on social media and engaging with your audience to nurture brand loyalty.

The Bottom Line:

Tracking KPIs and measuring the success of your social media efforts is essential for optimizing your strategy and achieving your business objectives. By defining your social media KPIs, measuring engagement, reach, conversions, and brand awareness metrics, and analyzing the data to glean actionable insights, you'll be better equipped to refine your strategy, drive meaningful results, and make a positive impact on your business. So, roll up your sleeves, dive into your social media analytics, and let's start measuring some success together!

Setting Up Social Media Dashboard: Tips for Monitoring Performance

Take control of your social media analytics and set up your very own performance dashboard! Let's dive into the world of analytics tools and dashboards and share some insider tips on how to monitor your performance metrics like a pro.

1. Choose the Right Analytics Tools:

The first step in setting up your social media dashboard is to choose the right analytics tools for your needs. There are plenty of options out there, from built-in analytics features on social media platforms to third-party tools like Google Analytics, Hootsuite, and Sprout Social. Take the time to research and evaluate different tools to find the ones that offer the features and capabilities you need to track your performance metrics effectively.

2. Identify Your Key Performance Metrics:

Next, you'll want to identify your key performance metrics – the specific data points that align with your business goals and indicate success. These could include engagement metrics like likes, comments, and shares, reach metrics like impressions and reach, conversion metrics like click-through rates and conversion rates, and brand awareness metrics like follower growth and mentions. By defining your key performance metrics upfront, you'll have a clear understanding of what you need to track and measure to evaluate the effectiveness of your social media efforts.

3. Set Up Custom Dashboards:

Once you've chosen your analytics tools and identified your key performance metrics, it's time to set up your custom dashboards. Most analytics tools allow you to create custom dashboards that display your performance metrics in a visually appealing and easy-to-understand format. Take advantage of this feature to create dashboards that are tailored to your specific needs and preferences. Organize your dashboards by platform, campaign, or metric type to make it easy to track and analyze your performance data at a glance.

4. Customize Your Reporting Periods:

When setting up your dashboards, be sure to customize your reporting periods to align with your reporting cadence and business goals. Whether you're tracking performance on a daily, weekly, monthly, or quarterly basis, choose reporting periods that give you meaningful insights into your performance trends and allow you to track progress over time. Many analytics tools offer customizable date ranges and reporting periods, so take advantage of these features to tailor your reporting to your needs.

5. Automate Data Collection and Reporting:

To streamline your monitoring process and save time, consider automating data collection and reporting wherever possible. Many analytics tools offer automated reporting features that allow you to schedule reports to be delivered to your inbox on a regular basis. Take advantage of these features to set up automated reports for your key performance metrics and dashboards, so you can stay informed about your performance without having to manually pull and analyze data.

Detailed Example: Imagine you're a marketing manager responsible for overseeing your company's social media strategy. You decide to set up a custom dashboard using Hootsuite to monitor performance metrics across all your social media channels. You create a dashboard that includes key performance metrics such as engagement (likes, comments, shares), reach (impressions, reach), conversion (click-through rates, conversion rates), and brand awareness (follower growth, mentions). You organize your dashboard by platform and campaign, with separate tabs for Facebook, Instagram, Twitter, and LinkedIn, as well as tabs for individual campaigns and initiatives. You customize your reporting periods to track performance on a monthly basis, with the option to drill down into daily or weekly data as needed. You schedule automated reports to be delivered to your inbox at the beginning of each month, so you can stay informed about your performance without having to log into the platform every day. With your custom dashboard set up, you can easily track and analyze your performance metrics, identify trends and opportunities, and make data-driven decisions to optimize your social media strategy for success.

The Bottom Line:

Setting up analytics tools and dashboards to monitor performance metrics is essential for evaluating the effectiveness of your social media efforts and making informed decisions to optimize your strategy. By choosing the right analytics tools, identifying your key performance metrics, setting up custom dashboards, customizing your reporting periods, and automating data collection and reporting, you'll be better equipped to track your performance metrics effectively and drive meaningful results for your business. So, roll up your sleeves, dive into your analytics tools, and let's start monitoring some performance metrics together!

Power of Data: Interpreting, Identify Trends, and Data-Driven Decisions

Hey there, data explorer! Ready to unlock the secrets hidden within your social media data and harness the power of insights to optimize your strategy? Well, you're in for a treat because we're about to dive into the world of data interpretation and show you how to identify trends and make data-driven decisions like a pro.

1. Understanding Your Data:

The first step in interpreting your data is to understand what it's telling you. Take the time to familiarize yourself with your performance metrics, dashboards, and reports, and learn how to interpret the data in the context of your business goals and objectives. Ask yourself questions like: What do these numbers mean? What trends or patterns do I see? How does this data align with my goals?

2. Look for Patterns and Trends:

Next, look for patterns and trends within your data that can provide valuable insights into your audience's behavior and preferences. Pay attention to recurring patterns, fluctuations, and anomalies in your performance metrics, and try to identify the underlying factors driving these trends. Look for correlations between different metrics and platforms, and consider how external factors like seasonality, holidays, or current events may be influencing your data.

Detailed Example: Imagine you're a social media manager for a fitness brand, and you're analyzing engagement metrics on your Instagram posts over the past year. As you review the data, you notice a consistent spike in engagement every Monday morning, coinciding with the start of the workweek. Digging deeper, you discover that posts featuring motivational quotes and workout tips perform particularly well on Mondays, resonating with your audience's desire for inspiration and motivation at the beginning of the week. Armed with this insight, you decide to capitalize on this trend by scheduling motivational posts for Monday mornings and tailoring your content strategy to align with your audience's behavior and preferences.

3. Identify Areas for Improvement:

Use your data analysis to identify areas for improvement and optimization within your social media strategy. Look for under-performing metrics or areas where you're not meeting your goals, and try to pinpoint the root causes of these issues. Are there specific types of content that consistently perform poorly? Are certain platforms or campaigns not delivering the results you expected? Use your data to diagnose the problem areas and brainstorm potential solutions to address them.

4. Make Data-Driven Decisions:

Armed with your insights and analysis, it's time to make data-driven decisions to optimize your social media strategy. Use your data to inform your decision-making process and guide your actions moving forward. Whether it's adjusting your content strategy, reallocating your budget, or refining your targeting tactics, let the data be your guide in making informed decisions that drive results and align with your business objectives.

Detailed Example: Continuing with the fitness brand example, let's say you notice that engagement on your Facebook ads promoting a new workout program is lower than expected. After analyzing the data, you discover that the targeting criteria for your ads are too broad, resulting in low relevance and engagement among your target audience. Based on this insight, you decide to refine your targeting strategy to focus on a more specific audience segment – fitness enthusiasts aged 25-35 who have expressed interest in similar workout programs. You also experiment with different ad creatives and messaging to better resonate with this audience segment. As a result, you see a significant increase in engagement and conversion rates, driving greater success for your ad campaign.

5. Iterate and Experiment:

Finally, don't be afraid to iterate and experiment based on your data analysis. The beauty of data-driven decision-making is that it allows you to continuously learn and improve over time. Use your data to test new ideas, strategies, and tactics, and measure the impact of these changes on your performance metrics. Be open to feedback, adapt to changing trends and preferences, and iterate your strategy based on what works best for your audience and your business goals.

The Bottom Line:

Interpreting data, identifying trends, and making data-driven decisions is essential for optimizing your social media strategy and driving meaningful results for your business. By understanding your data, looking for patterns and trends, identifying areas for improvement, making data-driven decisions, and iterating based on insights, you'll be better equipped to refine your strategy, maximize your impact, and achieve your goals. So, roll up your sleeves, dive into your data, and let's start making some data-driven decisions together!

Innovation: Continuous Experimentation, Testing, and Iteration

Embark on a journey of continuous experimentation and iteration to stay ahead of the curve in the ever-evolving landscape of social media marketing. You're in for an exciting ride because we're about to dive into the world of experimentation, testing, and iteration and share some best practices to help you innovate and thrive in the dynamic world of social media.

1. Embrace a Culture of Experimentation:

The first step in staying ahead of the curve is to embrace a culture of experimentation within your organization. Encourage your team to think outside the box, challenge assumptions, and explore new ideas and approaches to social media marketing. Create a safe environment where failure is seen as an opportunity to learn and grow, rather than a setback.

2. Test, Test, and Test Some More:

Testing is the key to innovation and improvement in social media marketing. Experiment with different content formats, messaging strategies, targeting tactics, and ad placements to see what resonates most with your audience. Use A/B testing, multivariate testing, and split testing to compare different variations of your campaigns and identify which performs best.

Detailed Example: Imagine you're a digital marketer launching a new ad campaign on Facebook to promote your latest product. Instead of sticking with your usual ad creative and messaging, you decide to experiment with different variations to see what drives the best results. You create three different versions of your ad – one featuring a product demonstration video, one highlighting customer testimonials, and one showcasing a limited-time offer. You launch all three ads simultaneously and monitor their performance over the course of a week. After analyzing the data, you discover that the ad featuring customer testimonials has the highest click-through rate and conversion rate, driving the most sales for your product. Encouraged by this success, you decide to incorporate more customer testimonials into your future ad campaigns to capitalize on their effectiveness.

3. Measure and Analyze Results:

Once you've conducted your experiments, it's essential to measure and analyze the results to glean insights and identify opportunities for improvement. Look at key performance metrics

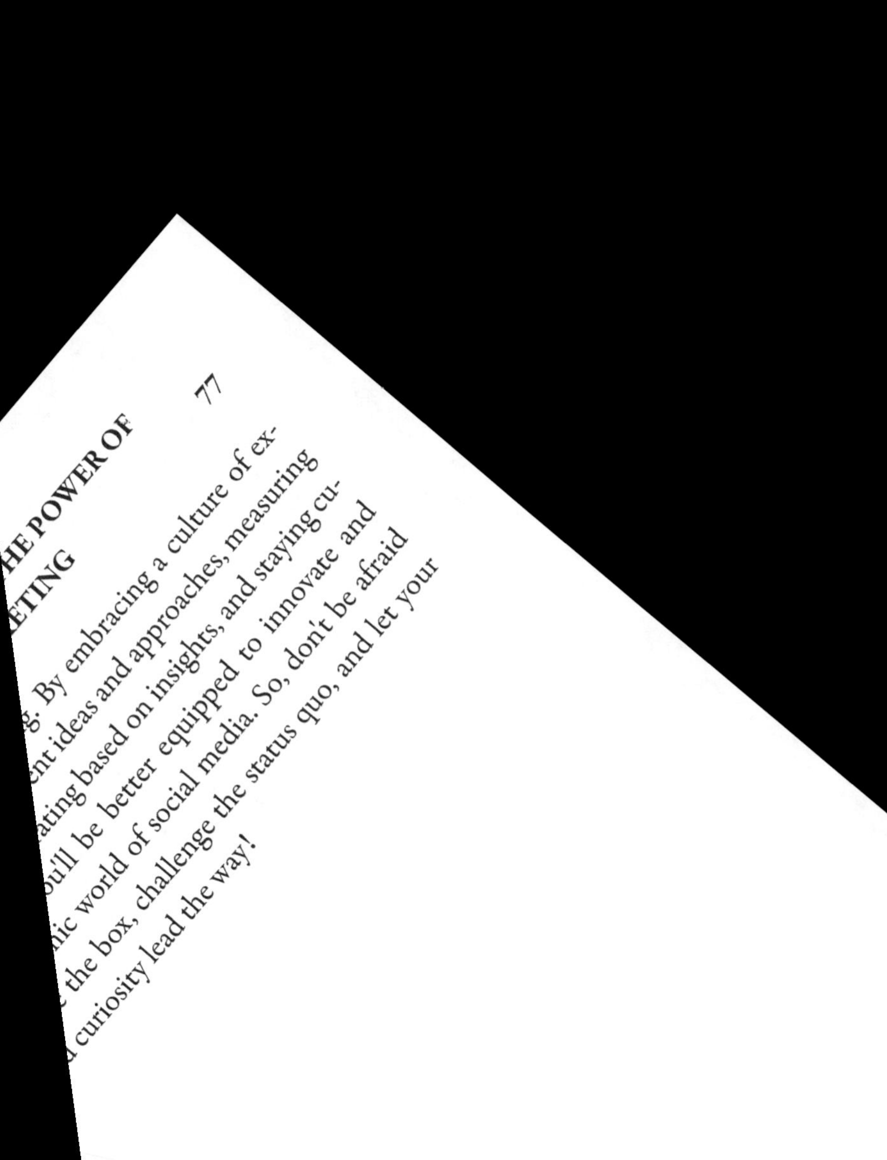

such as engagement, reach, conversions, and ROI to evaluate the success of your experiments. Pay attention to trends and patterns in the data, and use your findings to inform your future strategy and decision-making.

4. Iterate Based on Insights:

Armed with your insights and analysis, it's time to iterate and refine your social media strategy based on what you've learned. Take the findings from your experiments and apply them to future campaigns and initiatives. Continuously iterate on your content, messaging, targeting, and tactics to optimize performance and stay ahead of the curve.

Detailed Example: Let's say you're a social media manager for a fashion brand, and you've recently experimented with different posting times on Instagram to see when your audience is most active. After analyzing the data, you discover that your audience is most engaged with your content on weekday evenings between 7-9 PM. Armed with this insight, you decide to adjust your posting schedule to align with these peak engagement times, scheduling your posts for weekdays between 7-9 PM to maximize reach and impact.

5. Stay Curious and Adaptive:

Finally, remember to stay curious and adaptive i
proach to social media marketing. The landscap
evolving, with new platforms, trends, and tech
all the time. Stay informed about indust
an eye on what your competitors are
ing new strategies and tactics to stay

The Bottom Line:

Continuous experimentation, testing
sential for staying ahead of the curve in the

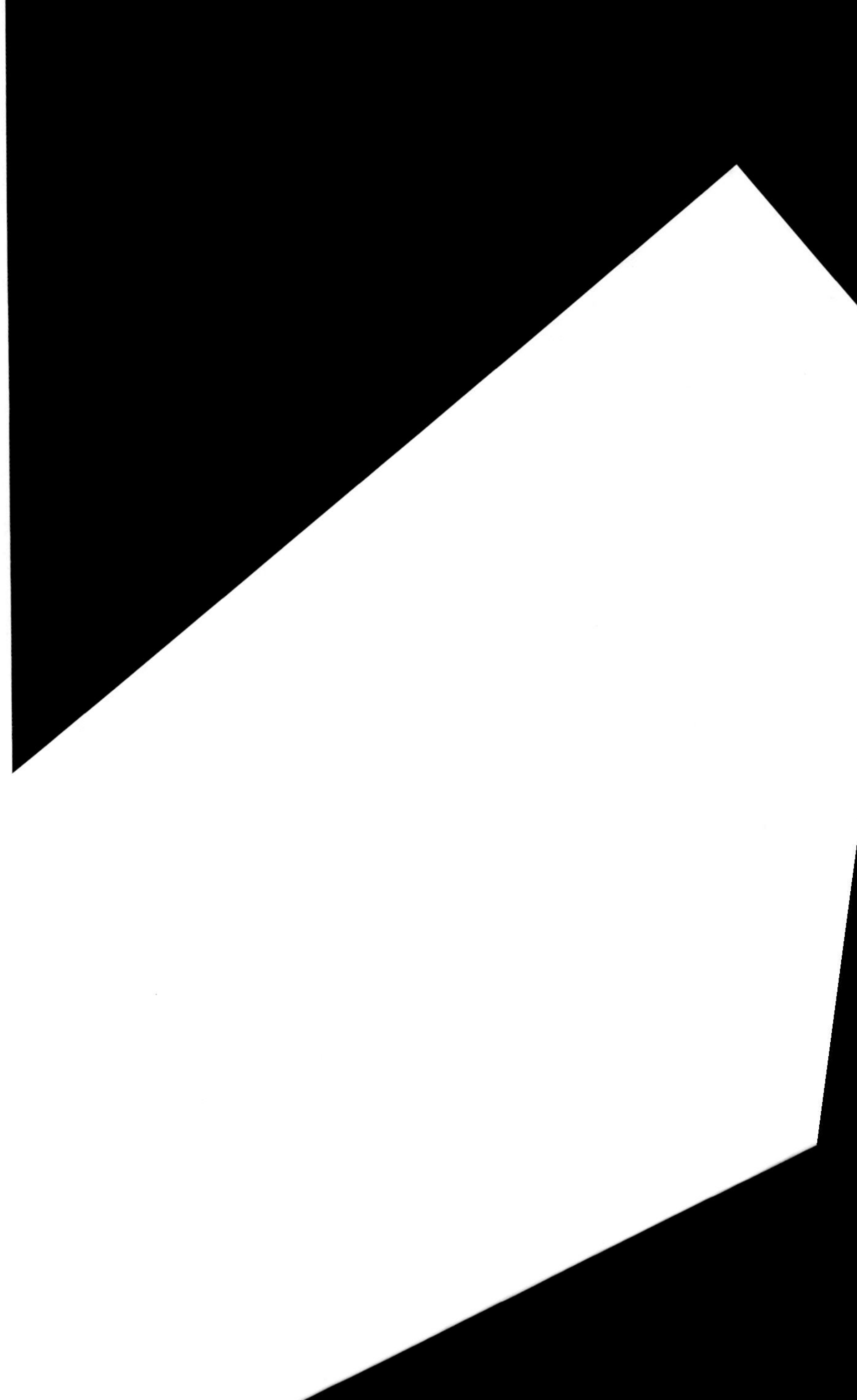